CW00499863

Your Marriage Shift

Your Marriage Shift

Kick Your Fears to the Curb, Avoid the Jokers and Smile Your Way to the Altar

Karen Oke

WINNERS
PRESS

Published in the United States by Winners Press, an imprint of Winners LLC, winnerspress.com.

ISBN: 979-8-9877517-7-0

Printed in the United States of America

Contents

Your Marriage Shift

Chapter 1

Lord, Will I Ever Find Someone to Love?

I wanted to be married, but scared to death does not look good in a wedding dress. Everywhere I looked, marriage seemed to be a game of roulette. In the media, we hear about so many celebrity marriages that start off all bright and starry-eyed but end in divorces with two black eyes – but it's not just celebs. Marriage, in general, is at an all-time low, with marriage rates taking suicide leaps and divorce rates sprinting to the finish line faster than Usain Bolt. Even among Christians, statistics show that marriage is no less vulnerable to failure.

Finding someone who won't break your heart or let you down can seem almost impossible. You want someone who sticks by you through thick and thin: someone you know will never hurt you or leave you when "for better or for worse" gets worse before it gets better, or there's more poorer than richer, or one or the other wants to cause the "'til death do us part." All these doubts and fears can make it hard to believe that there really is "the one" out there for you.

In my immediate family, all I saw was failed marriages on repeat. And in my own life, I could not see myself getting to the point of jumping the broom because my dating experience didn't offer much of anything but a broken, dusty broom that had been used too many times. I did not have a lot of boyfriends, which was fortunate because one encounter with the wrong one can be enough to ruin your perspective on what the right one is supposed to be like. I learned that the hard way.

I didn't know anything about dating or what to look for in a guy or relationship, so I got into a relationship by default. As the saying goes, when you don't stand for something, you'll fall for anything. But there's one thing about a woman: she can sense when something's off. The problem comes when she overrules that gut feeling by convincing herself that everything is okay or simply ignores it. That was the mistake I made: I knew something didn't feel right about connecting with this one particular guy, but I got involved anyway.

MARRIAGE SHIFT #1

Never put your internal alarm on snooze.

The relationship had been going on for months, and I thought it was going just as well for him as it was for me. I was in love, but apparently, I was in love all by myself. One joke that he did not find very funny was all it took for him to boot me out of his apartment and his life. There I was, thinking we would just talk about it later when things cooled down and make up. I never expected heartbreak to hit so suddenly when he called off our relationship out of the blue, leaving me with no explanation. But despite my hurt and confusion, I kept hoping we would get back together.

As hope faded, anger erupted. I would call him and yell at him and curse him out. Crazy! But the truth was I was in deep depression. On top of all that emotional drama, I had to deal with the humiliation of having to ask my mom to help me move my stuff out of my apartment and back into her place in upstate New York. Thank God I never moved in with him. I was dumb, but not that dumb.

Here's a wild but true story. After we broke up, my ex's mom gave me some crazy advice. She actually suggested that I wash my private parts and use that water to bring her son back. Yeah, I know; some seriously strange practices were going on there. What was I supposed to do, use the water to make iced tea and then invite him over for something cool to drink? Whatever she had in mind, I wasn't going for it!

As it turns out, she was a big fan of mine and obviously willing to resort to desperate measures to keep me and her son together. I was too good for him and she knew it, but she still wanted the best for him. I almost fell over when she gave me her "how to keep a man" strategy. I immediately shut down that crazy idea and told her, in as nice a way as possible, that I don't believe in that kind of stuff. I didn't want to offend her because, for all I knew, she might have had another "recipe" for ex-girlfriends who got on her bad side. The funny thing was that she had gone through multiple divorces, so her how-to-keep-a-man practices apparently hadn't helped her either.

Together or not, my ex and I still had mutual family connections. My family knew his family and vice versa, and I had relationships with some of his family members. So, when his father got sick with cancer, I went to visit him at the hospital. And who should I bump into? You guessed it: The Guy!

Any hope of me and The Guy getting back together went out the door when I looked up from his father's hospital bedside and saw him waltz in with his new girlfriend by his side. He knew how close I was to his family and must have realized the odds of my coming to see his father were high. He may have thought that if I saw him with someone else I could gain some kind of closure, but all that did was make things even more painful. That was it! My bubble burst with one brutal jab. It felt like the final nail in the coffin, even though the relationship was already over. It was a cruel testament to how quickly love can turn into hurt in an instant.

At first I felt angry and hurt, but eventually, I let go of these feelings realizing that sometimes love isn't enough if someone doesn't have the same level of commitment you do. So I did what any disillusioned woman would do when a man takes her heart and slams it into the concrete of disinterest: I decided to never date again. And as I worked through getting closure from that bad breakup, I realized how far I had drifted from my relationship with God. It was as though I had traded one relationship for the other, and they were mutually exclusive. It was God or The Guy; I never imagined I could have both.

MARRIAGE SHIFT #2

Anyone who makes you feel far away from God is someone you need to stay far away from.

Now, with The Guy out of the picture, I was free to turn my attention back to God. The only place I felt relief from my heartache was at church. So I joined the choir, started traveling on missions trips, and gradually deepened my relationship with God. He became my confidante, the only One I trusted enough to pour my broken heart out to.

One day, in one of our heart-to-heart talks, I made Him a promise.

"God, if you get me through this breakup, I will never stray away from you."

I kept that promise. I kept it when family pressured me about when I was going to find somebody and settle down. I kept it when I saw happy couples or friends hooking up and joyfully entering into celebratory engagements and marital bliss. I kept it when I had to take myself out to dinner or pop my own popcorn for my solo Netflix binges. I kept it because I did not want to experience that kind of hurt again or risk anyone coming between me and my renewed relationship with God. And then came White Socks.

White Socks was a guy I had gone to school with as a young girl back in Nigeria. We had two things in common: we were in the same class, and his mother was our teacher. I never thought of him as anything but a classmate. I gave him the nickname White Socks because his mother always kept his socks looking so clean. When I later migrated to Houston, White Socks wasn't even a memory for me. So, you can imagine my surprise when he slid into my DM years later. To make a long story short, we got reacquainted and started dating.

Isn't it funny how you can want to be with someone so bad, but they don't want you until they hear about or see you with someone else? That's what happened with The Guy. Things were going great between White Socks and me, and I was really into him. Then, out of the blue, I got a call from The Guy asking me out to dinner. He had broken up with his girlfriend and had an epiphany.

"I want us to get back together."

I could hardly believe what I was hearing. *This guy must have lost his kicked-me-out-of-his-life-for-no-reason mind*! Ah, *no*! That's not about to happen! Getting back with him was no longer an option under consideration. I'm not a vengeful person, but it sure felt good to inform him of my current situation.

"I'm already involved with someone else."

I had waited so long for him to tell me he wanted us to get back together that even my waiting had cobwebs on it. But I had long since dusted them off and finally moved on.

MARRIAGE SHIFT #3

If he left without a reason, don't let him come back with a reason.

When it comes to relationship heartache, few things can hurt worse than loving someone who doesn't love you back and just dumps you out of the blue. Navigating relationship heartbreak is no easy task, especially when you're left with no explanations and your ex appears to have moved on quickly, right in front of you. It will save you time to understand that time does *not* heal all wounds. You never "just get over it," and getting under the next one to try to get over the last one isn't the answer either.

Pain is a life lesson, not a life sentence. But to avoid it in the future, courage and honesty are required. You need courage to take a good hard look at more than *his* issues; you have to look at your own issues as well, ask yourself some hard questions, and give yourself honest answers. *What about me led me to choose him? Why did I stay as long as I did? Why would I want someone back who has proven to be no good for me?* In answering those questions, you will begin to find the answers to what needs to be worked out or worked on in your own life. Because when it comes right down to it, it's not about "him;" it's about you – your life, your future, and your decisions.

MARRIAGE SHIFT #4

When you're looking for someone to love, start with God and yourself.

The quality of our lives depends on our fulfillment of destiny, which is very much affected by who we choose for a spouse. I realized my relationship with The Guy pulled me away from God and, consequently, God's plan for my life, which is so dangerous. When I returned to God, everything got back in the right order. If I had married The Guy, I have no doubt my whole life would be a total mess! I wouldn't be doing the amazing destiny things I'm doing now, even experiencing the joys of motherhood as I do. Thank God that relationship ended! It hurt for a while, but not forever. Now I'm emotionally well and living my best life!

A lot of women are walking around with undiagnosed wounds and leprous hearts. Why do I say leprous? Because lepers have lost the ability to feel. As a result, they can be wounded and not realize it. The same can be true about your heart. You're fooling yourself when you exit a bad relationship and think there is nothing to heal. If you ever found yourself tripping emotionally over something small that happened in the relationship or mentally holding onto something from a past or current relationship for hours, days, or months, tormenting yourself about what you did wrong, then you definitely have some healing to do. Take some time to examine yourself for wounds, whether they were self-inflicted or inflicted by the person you were involved with. And *never* lie to yourself about the truth.

Loving unconditionally is a wonderful and even achievable ideal. However, you must understand that there is no unconditional love without pain. Even when you find the right person to be with, things will not be perfect. But by the same token, ongoing and persistent pain is a signal for change. It's a big red flashing neon sign telling you that the love you need is just not there. Run, do not walk, to the nearest exit, and *move on*!

MARRIAGE SHIFT #5

Take time to heal so you don't carry past pain into your future relationship.

Marriage isn't about the odds or statistics. It's about two people who genuinely love each other and want to build something together, who make a vow to stay together no matter what. But that "no matter what" should not be at the expense of your well-being. If you're fortunate enough to find someone who fulfills all of those conditions, marriage is definitely worth it.

My heart began to heal when I stopped worrying so much about why The Guy didn't want me and started trusting that God would bring me the right one at the right time – and He did. Now here I am, happily married with a loving husband by my side. So don't be discouraged if your dating life has been catastrophic. Don't give up just yet.

The good news is marriage is not a roll of the dice. With God's help and wisdom, you *can* find someone to love who will love you in return. There are still plenty of marriage success stories out there that demonstrate that even in an imperfect world, we can make it if we trust in God. So take courage, and keep hoping and believing you will find someone that is right for you in God's perfect timing. Now, I know that's more easily said than done, so let me tell you more about my story and the lessons I learned that helped me land safely in my own happily ever after.

A PRAYER FOR MY SINGLE SISTER ...

Dear God,

I come to You on behalf of my sister who needs healing from her past relationships. I pray that You instill in her the courage and strength to face her pain and find healing through Your divine love.

Please guide her toward the path of self-discovery, where she can learn to forgive herself and others and cultivate a deep sense of self-love and acceptance. Help her see that she is worthy of love and respect and that her past does not define her future.

May she be reminded of the words of Psalm 147:3, "He heals the brokenhearted and binds up their wounds." Let her experience Your healing touch and give her comfort through her struggles.

Guide her towards the right path where she can find the love and happiness she desires. Help her to trust in Your divine plan and timing and know that You have a perfect love story written just for her.

Give her the strength to let go of any bitterness or anger towards those who have hurt her. Help her to release her pain and surrender it to You, finding freedom in Your grace and mercy.

As she embarks on this journey of healing, may she always remember that she is never alone. Your love surrounds her each day, and You are always with her, guiding and protecting her every step of the way.

Amen.

SAY THIS TO YOURSELF:

I am worthy of love and respect, and my past does not define my future.

Chapter 2

It's Just A Piece of Paper, Right?

I started life in a daddy-less home, so my earliest memory of what a marriage looked like was written in disappearing ink. By the time I got old enough to spell 'relationship,' it looked like D-I-V-O-R-C-E. Unfortunately, my mother had a history of picking men who were either unripe or rotten to the core, and I was afraid of making the same mistakes. I did not want her history of divorces to become my own.

After the bad breakup with The Guy, I just didn't trust myself to make the right choice when it came to picking a man. I couldn't afford to bounce from one bad relationship to the next. It would have taken too much out of me, and I didn't want to have to gather the pieces of me to present when the right one came along. So, I prayed.

"Lord, I need you to pick for me. I'm not good at dating; I don't trust myself. I need You to drop my husband in my lap!"

Then I waited. No, seriously – I waited. Everybody

thought I was crazy. Sometimes I questioned my own sanity. I mean, who makes a request like that and actually believes it will happen? But I was crazy enough to believe it would. And you know what? I would rather look crazy than end up in a crazy relationship with some crazy joker. And I know I'm not the only one.

MARRIAGE SHIFT #6

It's better to be single and crazy about marriage than to go crazy trying to get out of one.

A lot of people are jaded when it comes to relationships, especially marriage. Being boo'd up for years with a ring on the wrong finger is trending. Some women have exchanged single "interested in men" statuses for "situationships" and "it's complicated."

Fear has become the new engagement ring. People are afraid of picking the wrong one and ending up with someone they don't or can't trust or being used for their money. Bad experiences, family legacies of breakups and divorce, and questions like "Why do I need to get married?" have colored us scared. Many have reasoned themselves out of the kind of commitment that is sealed in ink and filed on public record. After all, "it's just a piece of paper," right?

Let's be real: getting a driver's license is far more difficult and requires much more preparation than getting a marriage license. Still, we hardly think twice about going after a driver's license. In fact, most people make getting a driver's license a goal. So why do some people shy away from getting a marriage license yet go after the more difficult process of getting a driver's license? I think we need to park here and talk about that for a minute.

Have you ever really thought about the ordeal of getting a driver's license? You think it's just a matter of filling out a few forms and taking a couple of tests, right? Wrong! First, you need to meet the minimum requirements set by the Department of Motor Vehicles (the dreaded DMV). You can't even apply for a driver's license unless you're at least a certain age. You have to study the driver's manual and be familiar with the specific rules and regulations for driving, as well as information about road signs, traffic laws, and safe driving practices. Then, before you can get a full driver's license, you typically need to get a learner's permit. To do this, you need to pass a written knowledge test at your local DMV office to make sure you understand the traffic laws, road signs, and safe driving practices. Who knows what a safe "stopping distance" is anyway? Some states even require a vision test. If you manage to pass the written test, once you have your learner's permit, you need to practice driving under the supervision of a licensed adult driver. And it doesn't end there.

When you apply for your driver's license, you must provide specific documents to verify your identity, residency, and legal presence in the United States. Suddenly, you need a utility bill, a birth certificate from the hospital (not just the state-issued one), and a blood sample from your great-great-grandmother. (I'm just kidding; you don't really need a blood sample.)

Finally, after weeks of studying, practicing, and panicking, the big day arrives, and you get behind the wheel for your driving test. It's basically like being in a Hollywood action movie! You have to swerve to avoid fake pedestrians and navigate an obstacle course of safety cones. But when you hear the words "you passed," it's a feeling like no other. It's like earning a badge of honor that says, "I can drive without crashing!"

On the other hand, with a marriage license, there's no mandatory studying or preparation, no one checks your vision, no assessment of your understanding of the knowledge required to have a safe, crash-free marriage, and no adult supervision is required. It's even cheaper to get a marriage license: $50 to $200 for a driver's license versus $25 to $115 for a marriage license. So, why do people burn with anticipation to get their driver's license but get ice blocks in their shoes when they think of getting a marriage license? One requires parallel parking skills, the ability to decipher confusing road signs, and the fine motor skills of a surgeon. The other requires *love*. Sure, you might have to call six different government offices to fill out the right paperwork, but at least you're not being asked to parallel park in front of a tight-lipped instructor who is scribbling on a clipboard. Plus, you can drive in the carpool lane for life!

MARRIAGE SHIFT #7

It's easier to get a marriage license than a driver's license.

We'll get a license for a gun, a license for our business, or a driver's license, but some will slam on the brakes when it comes to a license for marriage. Why? It all boils down to one word: *commitment.*

Marriage is a big commitment, and it can be intimidating to even think of taking such a big step. You may find yourself asking, "Do I really want to commit to this person for the rest of my life?" That question can be especially daunting if you are a single Christian woman who wants to be married. For one thing, you may not be able to jump in and out of marriage so easily if it doesn't work out when the church and God are involved. But why does marriage scare people so much? Let's explore some of the reasons.

Conditioning

Whether we realize it or not, we've been brainwashed to be scared of marriage without even realizing it. The language some use to describe marriage is so negative it's insane! But it's so subtle you might not have noticed. Let me break it down for you using some of the more common phrases for describing married life.

Ball and Chain. Seriously? Imagine being chained to a heavy iron ball and dragging it around, struggling to move freely. That's how some people think of marriage. They see it as a burden that restricts their freedom, like a prisoner in shackles. 'Ball and chain' suggests that marriage is a source of frustration. But how on God's green earth did we end up using it to describe marriage?

One theory is that the term comes from the practice of chaining prisoners together with a heavy iron ball and chain as a form of punishment. The weight and constraint of the ball and chain made it difficult for prisoners to move around freely or escape, just as some people believe that marriage can restrict their freedom and independence.

Another theory is that the phrase comes from the practice of chain gangs in the southern United States, where prisoners were forced to do manual labor while chained together. The heavy ball and chain on their ankles made it difficult to run away or move quickly, just as some people believe that marriage can be a burden that holds them back.

'Ball and chain' is a negative and outdated way of referring to marriage that perpetuates harmful stereotypes about what marriage is all about. Marriage is a fulfilling and positive experience for many people, and it's important to recognize and celebrate its value and importance in our society. But let's dig a little deeper to see more ways we've been conditioned without our permission.

Tied down: Everything about this screams bondage! When we hear someone referring to marriage as being "tied down," it is usually associated with something negative – a limitation or loss of freedom. Being 'tied down' suggests that being married restricts your ability to do what you want or go where you want. Sadly, that's a common sentiment when it comes to marriage. Society has conditioned us to believe that being married means sacrificing our independence, our dreams, and our individuality. But what if we flipped the script? What if we saw commitment in marriage as something that actually frees us to be our best selves? I hear you. You're saying, Karen, I know you wrote a book and everything, but how do you figure marriage can free me to be my best self? Well, I'm glad you asked.

I'll be the first to admit that as wonderful as marriage is, it can sometimes seem daunting and overwhelming, especially in a world where we are constantly bombarded with negative portrayals of relationships. The idea of sacrificing our independence or losing our sense of self can be terrifying. Still, I'm here to tell you that marriage can actually be the key to unlocking your full potential and becoming your most authentic self.

First and foremost, having a supportive spouse can be a game-changer. When you have someone who believes in you and encourages you to pursue your dreams, it can give you the push you need to take risks and try new things. Your spouse can be your biggest cheerleader, helping you overcome struggles and celebrating your successes with you. Now, that's what I call *really* being boo'd up!

Shared responsibilities are another benefit of marriage. When you have someone to help share the load of chores, bills, and other mundane tasks, you can free up your time and energy to focus on other things that truly matter to you. (Can I get a whoop-whoop for not having to take out the trash?) Seriously, whether it's pursuing a hobby, starting a business, or going back to school, having a spouse who helps lighten the load can make all the difference.

But I believe the most liberating part of marriage is the personal growth and perspective it offers. Being in a committed relationship requires vulnerability, communication, and reasonable compromise. These skills not only strengthen your relationship but also carry over into other areas of your life, making you a better friend, daughter, sister, and colleague. Marriage can teach you to be more empathetic, patient, and understanding, qualities that will serve you well in all aspects of your life.

MARRIAGE SHIFT #8

If it feels like a trap, don't take the bait.

Don't let fear hold you back from experiencing the limitless opportunities that come with being in a committed, loving relationship. Trust that you'll find a partner who will support you, challenge you, and help you become the best version of yourself. Marriage isn't a trap but rather a chance to soar. But, speaking of traps, let's look at a couple more terms that sabotage our marriages before they even get a chance to start.

Trap: You might be okay with this word if you're talking about a genre of music, but otherwise, everything about the word makes you want to run in the opposite direction. Viewing marriage as a trap implies that marriage is a deceitful or insidious way of trapping someone into a commitment they may not want. Referring to marriage in terms like this gives it a bad rap.

Back in the day, marriage was often seen as an institution where societal norms and expectations pushed people, especially women, to get married for various reasons such as financial security, family alliances, or to fulfill gender-specific roles like childbearing and housekeeping. In that context, some individuals, especially those who felt pressured or forced into marriage, may have used the term "trap" to express their discontent and the feeling of being caught in a commitment they did not desire or fully consent to.

Well, excuse my English, but marriage ain't what it used to be, and that's a good thing! Attitudes about marriage have changed. Nowadays, in many cases, the idea of marriage aligns with the blueprint God intended: a consensual union of two individuals based on love, respect, and shared values. So, we need to kick the old "trap" mentality to the curb!

'Trap,' as it relates to marriage, is a reminder of the past; it does not need to be an indicator of your future. I believe you're starting to see how we've been programmed to fear the commitment of marriage. Let's look at one more example to drive the point home.

Settling down: Just pause for a minute and look at the two words that make up that phrase: *settling* and *down*. I mean, come on! Those words are not doing marriage any favors. Who wants to associate their happily ever after with settling and down? While the phrase is not necessarily negative on its own, in the context of marriage, it sounds like the end of all things exciting and adventurous. No, thank you! We need to find a better way to describe the beauty of lifelong commitment.

MARRIAGE SHIFT #9

Marriage is not about settling down but rising up.

At the root of this fear of commitment is exactly that: *fear*! And to overcome fear, it's important to take the time to understand what's causing it. In addition to the subtle programming of our minds against marriage, the fear of commitment can stem from many different sources: past heartbreaks, a fear of losing control, or a fear of making the wrong decision, just to name a few. If you find yourself feeling hesitant at the thought of marriage, take some time to reflect on where your fear is coming from so that you can address it directly.

Fear of the Unknown

One reason marriage might seem scary is because it is an unknown. Sometimes it's hard to imagine what lies ahead in a lifelong partnership, and that can lead to fear and uncertainty. *What if I don't know how to handle certain situations? What if things don't work out between us?* These questions can cause anxiety and make it difficult for some people to take the plunge into marriage. I get it.

However, you can find hope and encouragement knowing that God has a plan for your life and will guide you through every step of the journey. By trusting in His infinite wisdom and embracing the opportunities for growth, love, and partnership that marriage can offer, you can overcome your fears and live a fulfilling life with a loving partner by your side.

Fear of Not Being Good Enough

Another common fear many women have about marriage is not feeling good enough for their partner or being afraid they won't be able to meet their future spouse's expectations. Let me tell you, it's easy to get caught up in comparing yourself with other women or even with your own expectations of what a "perfect" wife should be like. This can cause feelings of inadequacy and insecurity.

Remind yourself that everyone has different needs when it comes to marriage. So it's important not to compare yourself to anyone or judge yourself harshly. Your marriage would not be like anyone else's because it involves two unique individuals: you and the person who marries you. Focus on meeting your own partner's needs instead of worrying about what someone else's marriage might look like. You might not be good enough for someone else's marriage, but you are definitely good enough for your own.

Fear of Losing Yourself

Some women have a fear of losing themselves after they get married, especially if they've been single for a long time. They worry that they will no longer be able to do all the things they enjoy doing, such as traveling or pursuing hobbies, without a partner's permission or approval. But I'm here to tell you that's not the case.

Freely sharing your interests and preferences is necessary for establishing a solid foundation for your marriage. When it comes right down to it, marriage has a lot to do with finding a happy middle ground. Compromise is the name of the game – not in the sense of lowering your standards or giving up your non-negotiables but looking for ways that work for both of you. It is possible.

Let me drop a truth bomb on you: fear is like mold. As long as it's kept in the dark, it continues to grow. But once you bring it out into the light, it's game over! The light is truth, and that truth is found in God's design for marriage. Now, let's be real – it's totally normal to feel nervous about getting married, even when you are convinced that the person you intend to marry is God's absolute best for you. But here's the thing: fear has no place in any relationship. If fear is hanging around, it means truth hasn't been properly introduced into the equation.

MARRIAGE SHIFT #10

Fear closes the door to an open mind.

Even the best relationships have their ups and downs; these are facts, and facts have no feelings. But if you know anything about an EKG, ups and downs are a sign of life. If there are no ups and downs, the relationship is flatlining. In other words, if everything is *always* smooth sailing, somebody is probably lying, and the marriage may be dying.

Marriage offers enough wonderful opportunities that come along with being in a committed relationship that make it worth embracing. So what can you do if you're feeling intimidated or afraid about committing to marriage? Bring those fears out of the shadows and let the truth shine on them. When God is invited into your journey, He helps you remove all the guesswork. You need the assurance that Someone bigger than both of you can guide you along the way.

Let me also say singlehood is not bad; it's just a different state of being. Learning to be happy and content in your single state is important so that a spouse becomes an addition rather than an obsession. When desire turns into obsession, it produces unrealistic expectations and puts a lot of pressure on a spouse. I refuse that on your behalf.

Finding the right spouse is not always an easy thing, but God is the ultimate matchmaker. So, walk with me into this next chapter, and we'll answer some of the hard questions about marriage using His perspective. Buckle up, keep an open mind, and get ready to discover the transformative power of faith in your quest for love. The answers will bring you closer to your future spouse and to God Himself.

A PRAYER FOR MY SINGLE SISTER ...

Dear God,

I come to You today on behalf of my sister who is struggling with the fear of committing to marriage. I pray that You give her the courage and strength to trust in Your plan for her life and to let go of her fears.

Remind her of Your infinite wisdom and guidance when it comes to matters of the heart. Help her to see that You have a perfect plan for her life and that whatever path she takes, You'll never leave her stranded at the side of the road.

Give her comfort in knowing that she will never be alone in her struggles; You will be with her every step of the way. Your love surrounds her each day, and You have a plan for her that is good and full of hope. Remind her of Your words from Jeremiah 29:11, "For I know the plans I have for You," declares the Lord, "plans to prosper You and not to harm You, plans to give You hope and a future."

As she navigates through this season of her life, help her to see marriage not as a source of fear but as an opportunity for growth, love, and partnership. May she be encouraged by Your words from Ecclesiastes 4:9-10, "Two are better than one because they have a good return for their labor: If either of them falls down, one can help the other up."

Finally, I pray that You remind her of her worth and that she is fearfully and wonderfully made in Your image. Let her always know that she is loved beyond measure by You and that Your love will never fail.

Amen.

SAY THIS TO YOURSELF:

I trust God's plan for my life and let go of all my fears.

Chapter 3

What's God Got to Do with It?

It's a good thing God doesn't have an account on Instagram, Snapchat, or Twitter! Sometimes it seems like there are stories of breakups everywhere you look on social media. Kanye and Kim – well, I think most people saw that one coming eventually. It still struck a chord, though. And when twin Tia Mowry of *Sister Sister* fame announced to her 12-million plus Instagram followers that she and hubby decided to go their separate ways, one follower voiced the heart of countless single women:

"Whyyyyy? I loved you guys together. *You were my last hope in love.* Fourteen years married, twenty-one years together. Come on, at least give us an explanation as to whyyyyy. *That's the longest relationship I have ever witnessed.*"

It's a sad commentary when people feel the need to look at a 6.7-inch LED screen to find marital inspiration only to be disappointed in 2,200 characters or less. But I'm here to tell you that despite all the negative press, God started the marriage project, and He wasn't counting on anyone's likes or comments to make it work. He set it up as an act of love between a man and a woman who did not have a plan B anywhere in sight.

MARRIAGE SHIFT #11

When you want to know how marriage works, check the Manufacturer's guide instead of social media likes.

God designed marriage to last a lifetime, but sometimes people sign on the dotted line before they read *and* understand the Manufacturer's instructions. This is why I believe so strongly in making sure any relationship you pursue has His blessing first.

So, how do you get God's blessing first? Well, let me start by saying that standing at the altar and hearing the preacher pronounce, "What God has joined together, let no man put asunder," does not mean the union is blessed. God's blessing does not come at the altar; it comes in the Garden. Now, grab yourself some tea while I take you all the way back to the beginning and explain what I mean.

If you've ever read the book of Genesis in the Bible, you've seen the account of how God created Adam and then Eve. Now, I'm not about to turn this book into a Bible study, but I do want to point out something many people overlook in the whole marriage account. We read (in Genesis Chapter 2) that God formed the woman while Adam was completely unaware that he even needed a wife. Adam was fast asleep (just like some of the men you might meet or maybe already have). Then, after the man wakes up, God brings the woman to him.

MARRIAGE SHIFT #12

If he's still "sleeping," he's not ready.

When Adam sees the woman, he immediately recognizes, *hey, I'm missing something, and this woman's got what I need!* He then spouts off the now infamous words that have since been repeated in over 100 translations. I'll put it in the VOICE translation to make sure you "hear" it loud and clear:

> **Adam**: At last, a suitable companion, a perfect partner.
> Bone from my bones. Flesh from my flesh.
> I will call this one "woman" as an eternal reminder
> that she was taken out of man. Now this is the reason
> a man leaves his father and his mother, and is united
> with his wife; and the two become one flesh.

- Genesis 2:23-24

And just like that, marriage is instituted.

Here's the point I want to make. In Adam's recognition of Eve as his wife – i.e., what he recognized as missing from his life – not once is 'love' mentioned. I hear you, *But don't you need love to make a marriage work?* Yes, you do, but it's not the fluffy, get 1,000,000 likes on social media kind of love that some women think of, want, or expect when it comes to marriage.

Love — the right kind of love — is a crucial ingredient in a relationship. However, it's not the driving force behind a successful marriage, especially as it relates to understanding what a woman needs most as a wife. Let me not jump the gun because before you can understand what a woman needs most as a wife, I have to say something about what a man needs most as a husband.

I've seen and heard of women bending over backward, trying to get a man to love them. Your hips, lips, and fingertips may catch a man's eye, but it takes more than that to hold his attention. Love does not sustain a marriage. Knowledge sustains a marriage, and that knowledge – or lack thereof – informs the decisions that are made. That's why you can have two people standing in front of a preacher saying they are in love one day and standing before a judge filing for divorce three months, six months, or a year later.

MARRIAGE SHIFT #13

A successful marriage is built in the boardroom, not the bedroom.

You might love flying in an airplane, but that does not mean you know how to be a pilot. To pilot a plane, you need *knowledge.* And just because you love somebody and get married to them, that does not mean the marriage will automatically work. Understanding that can make the difference between cruising in your marriage at a high altitude or crash landing. *You need knowledge.* We'll talk more about it in the next chapter, but for now, let's get back to understanding what a man needs most as a husband. So, back to Genesis.

According to God's design for marriage, before a man can recognize a woman as a wife, he needs to be doing something purposeful. Every man who realizes his need for a wife will identify the right woman as a "suitable companion." This is where you need to ask, *suitable for what*? I'm glad you asked, and the answer in one word is *purpose.*

One of the biggest mistakes women make, which has caused frustration, separation, and devastation in many marriages, is this: they marry a man for his *potential. Scrrreeeeech*! Slam on the brakes right here, and write this down somewhere in permanent ink: never, *ever* marry a man for his *potential.*

MARRIAGE SHIFT #14

Don't marry for potential. Marry for purpose.

I've seen and met women who married their husbands because of the potential they saw in them, and twenty years into the marriage, they're *still* waiting for that potential to be fulfilled. Remember, a man needs a *suitable companion*, or, as some translations put it, a suitable "*helper*" for a wife.

Before we go any further, throw away any mental images of Viola Davis in a maid's uniform – *You is kind. You is smart. You is important.* Yes, you are, but that's not the kind of helper we're talking about. Come back to Adam.

Before Eve was even a thought, when it was just God and Adam walking and talking in the Garden, God gave Adam something to *do*. God said, *look here, Adam, this Garden is not going to weed itself. You're going to have to take care of all this! There's land to farm, animals to care for, and fruit to harvest. You've got work to do!*

MARRIAGE SHIFT #15

If he doesn't have (or want) a job, don't give him a nod.

Let me quickly add a point for clarity, just to make sure we're on the same page. I'm not talking about a guy who's going through a transition period, or attending school, or starting their own business, or changing careers. No, no. I'm talking about one of those jokers who's got a knack for being jobless.

Before a man can recognize his need for a suitable companion or *helper*, he should be *doing* something that necessitates that help. Seems so simple when you read it in black and white, but so many women miss it right there. God told Adam to work the ground. In other words, God gave Adam something to *manage*. If there is nothing for a man to manage or do, there is nothing for the woman to help him with. No man needs help doing nothing. He can do nothing all by himself!

MARRIAGE SHIFT #16

If he can't manage a job, bills, or himself, he can't manage a marriage.

You see, Adam did not wait until Eve came along to start doing what he was supposed to do; nope, he didn't. When

Eve was led to Adam, he was already busy doing what he was supposed to do, which was to manage the Garden and everything in it. That is why she could step right into her role as a suitable helper and start helping him with what he was already doing. That's what we as women are called, made, and formed to do as wives.

God invested a *lot* in a woman to have the title of a suitable helper. He made her the missing piece to the right man's puzzle – she *complements* his life. I don't want you to gloss over that. Let me remind you that Adam was not in the Garden by himself. God was his companion. But God looked at Adam and said, *I'm God, and I'm all that, but this man needs someone else besides Me*! Do you see how outstanding you are and how significant God deems you to be as a woman and potential wife? Girl, you are *all* that!

A wife is there to bring everything that she is to the marriage to help her husband with what he is supposed to be doing as a man. Gone are the days when a woman sits around waiting for some knight in shining armor to come along and "rescue" her from her singlehood. Your singlehood is the time you are establishing yourself as the suitable, perfect partner. I've met women whose main ambition is to marry a man who's got money. But just in case you know someone like that, please let them know that rich men who are serious about marriage look for rich women or women who at least have a similar mindset when it comes to money and wealth.

What a man needs the most is not someone to warm his bed at night, cook his meals, and provide a soft place for his head to rest. What he needs the most is a *suitable helper* who can help him fulfill his *purpose*. That proves how powerful a wife is, which brings me to my next point.

Let me explain it this way. When God brought Eve to Adam, it was not a simple equation of one plus one equals two as most couples believe, because a woman is an *incubator*. An incubator takes what you put in it and causes it to grow; it maintains the optimal temperature and environment for growth. It also protects against excessive noise and other outside agents that would cause harm to what's growing inside. That means a woman does not add to whatever a man gives her; because she is an incubator, she *multiplies* it and causes it to grow.

A wife is an incubator by God's design. That's why if a man gives his wife groceries, she will give him a meal. If he gives her a house, she will make a home out of it. But if he gives her trouble, she will give him a multiplicity of trouble to deal with. A man needs to make sure he gives his woman (wife) good things so that she can multiply those good things, and together, they produce better things than they would if they were both single. See how that works?

This is very important because when a man doesn't understand this and brings nothing to the table for the woman to help him with, guess what? She will have to multiply and give back to him? Nothing! And nothing multiplied by nothing equals nothing, and that's a formula for an empty, unproductive marriage.

So, what does a man need most in a marriage? He needs a suitable helper, that perfect partner who will help him accomplish his purpose. On the other hand, what a woman needs most is a man who understands what that purpose is. She needs him to have a *vision* for their life together. Otherwise, this is one way a marriage can fail before it even starts. Let me explain.

If a man comes into a relationship but he doesn't even have a vision for the woman to help him with, she cannot fulfill her role as a suitable helper because there is nothing for her to incubate and multiply. So, if that man can't lay out the vision for where he's taking the woman, he will frustrate her role as a suitable helper. And she – with her incubator self – will multiply frustration and give it back to him. That's why it's essential for a man to know where he's going. If he doesn't have a plan, map, or vision, he will fail the woman.

MARRIAGE SHIFT #17

Love is not blind. It sees and follows a clear vision.

Now, when I speak of vision, I'm not talking about a man having a business. A vision is not about a man having a company or being a CEO. All of that is good, but a vision is much more than that. When I talk about having a vision, I'm referring to the man having a vision for the *relationship*. As a man, where does he plan for your relationship to be two, five, or ten years from now?

When a man has a vision and knows what he wants, he

can plan ahead and say this is what I want for my wife, this is what I want for my children, this is what I want for us as a couple. This is the business I want us to get into two years from now; this is the company I want us to have five years down the road. So, it's more than business. The man can be working, and the woman can be working, but the man needs to have a vision.

You must understand that because a wife is a suitable helper, she wants to support her husband. In fact, she is called, appointed, and anointed to support her husband. But she cannot support something that she doesn't understand. So, a husband or husband-to-be needs to let his wife or wife-to-be know where they are going so that she can support him in the vision as they carry it out together.

Look, if you're going to be some fortunate man's ride or die as his wife, you should know exactly where you're riding to and, if you really had to die, what you would be dying for. Doesn't that make sense?

A wife is God's investment in a marriage. Read that again. She is her husband's "talent." That may not make much sense to you if you've never read the Parable about the Talents (Matthew 25:14-30). Just in case you haven't read it, let me quickly paraphrase it for you.

Three men are given something valuable to invest. What they were given varied based on their individual capabilities to take care of what they received. Each man was expected to take what he was given, recognize its value, and maximize its profitability. In other words, there was supposed to be a return on the investment. Well, two of the men understood what they had and why they had it and took the investment and produced a return. But the other guy treated what he was given like it had no value at all and buried it.

This happens in many relationships when the man fails to recognize the value of the woman that comes into his life. I know I've got an 'amen' out there somewhere. That's why that knucklehead didn't know what to do with you. He couldn't recognize your value, so he treated you like dirt, buried your value, and the relationship could not produce anything.

That's what happens when a woman hooks up with a man who lacks vision – a plan for where they're going in the relationship: he will bury her value as a suitable helper by keeping her in a place where she can't be productive and produce a return. I guarantee there'll be no joy in such a marriage.

Let me say it one more time for the ones in the back. A man needs a clear picture of where he's going, where he's taking the relationship, and his plans for the future. Otherwise, if he has no vision, he will frustrate the woman's role as a suitable helper who was crafted specifically by God to help him. This is why choosing the right life partner for marriage is so important, and that's impossible without God's involvement.

MARRIAGE SHIFT #18

Marriage should increase your value, not bury it.

You cannot afford to leave God out of the equation when it comes to marriage. Number one: He's the *creator* of it, so if you want it to work, you'll need to follow the Manufacturer's instructions. Number two: He's the Father of the Bride, the One who *invests* His daughter in the right marriage so she can help to make it productive.

To embark on the journey of marriage without God's input is like eating fast food while you're running on a treadmill. The only thing you'll do is wear yourself out. You'll get nowhere, and you'll never see the results you're after. But when you do it His way, I am a living testimony that this thing *works*! I am *very* happily married, and you can be too! But I did not get here because I did everything right.

As we move forward in *Your Marriage Shift*, there's a not-so-little something we need to address – realistic expectations in marriage. This is a topic that often gets swept under the rug, like those crumbs you pretend not to see after a late-night snack. In this next chapter, we're going to get realer (if it's a word in Scrabble, I can use it too) – like *really* real. We're going to do the cupid shuffle all over those rose-colored glasses that mislead women into thinking that a great marriage has to be flawless. So get your slingshot ready because we're about to take some giant marriage killers down!

A PRAYER FOR MY SINGLE SISTER ...

Dear God,

I come to You on behalf of my single sister who wants a marriage after Your own design. I pray that You give her wisdom as she navigates the complex world of relationships and meets and interacts with new people. Open her eyes to recognize the kind of man who appreciates her value and is prepared to treat her as Your investment in their marriage.

Strengthen her spirit to discern between what is fleeting and what aligns with Your purpose for her life. Give her the strength not to compromise or settle for less than Your best for her. Fill her heart with patience and peace, knowing that You are the ultimate orchestrator of love and companionship.

Thank You for Your abundant grace and blessings in her life, and I know that You have even greater blessings in store for her future. As she moves towards the fulfillment of her desire for marriage, remind her that she brings favor to her husband and value to anything she's a part of.

I affirm Your promise over her life that whoever has the privilege of finding her finds a good, excellent, understanding, valuable partner who brings Your special favor to the marriage.

Amen.

SAY THIS TO YOURSELF:

I am a valuable and worthy woman. I bring favor and excellence to any relationship I am involved in.

Chapter 4

What Mom 'n 'Em Never Told You

"If you never had a happy marriage, you can't tell me nothin' about marriage!"

That is one of the most nonsensical statements I have ever heard, and I've heard it more than a few times! Listen, there are two ways you can learn wisdom: from your own experience or from someone else's experience. So, don't be too quick to dismiss people who made a wreck of their own marriages *and* have learned from their mistakes. Joining in marriage with someone you can love for a lifetime is more than just knowing what you want; you also need to be sure of what you *don't* want. That's also wisdom.

I learned a lot about marriage from watching my mother's example. Her experiences taught me enough to know what I *did not* want for my own marriage. I didn't want it to end in divorce. I didn't want my children to grow up in a fatherless home. I did not want to fail before I even started because of jaded genes, faded dreams, and false expectations.

Much of what we're taught through mainstream media sets us up for failure in our relationships. It starts when we're little girls, reading or being read fairy tales, where everybody but the witch has a flawless complexion, never ages, and always, *always* ends up with Prince Charming in the end. *Snow White*, *Sleeping Beauty*, and *Cinderella* have subtly conditioned our hearts for the possibility of "... happily ever after. The end." Am I suggesting that you cannot have a fantastic marriage where you can joyfully fulfill your purpose and help your husband fulfill his? Of course not. I'm here to let you know you can have all that and more! I'm also here to point out the traps and pitfalls that can trip you up before you ever walk down the aisle. Let me start with "the one."

Make no mistake about it: I am convinced that my husband is God's perfect will for me, but there's one caveat: the way my husband and I came together was definitely more the exception than the rule. I don't want you to think the way things happened for me is a formula for you to follow. But I promised in an earlier chapter to tell you more about how my husband (aka White Socks) and I came together.

I shared before how White Socks and I met as schoolmates back in Nigeria and that when I came to the United States, I wasn't thinking about White Socks any more than I was the man on the moon. But I went to a prayer meeting one night, and everything changed. I was there, but not there because I was preoccupied in my mind. It was one of those times when I was struggling on the inside wondering when or *if* I would ever meet someone I could love and who would love me back. Then one of the pastors came over to pray for me.

I had never spoken with this man, and as far as I knew, he knew nothing about me or my life. So I was expecting a generic "bless her, Lord" kind of prayer. But all of a sudden, he stopped praying and looked me straight in the eyes.

"A year from now, you will meet your husband." Before I could process what he had just said, he continued, "He is somebody you already know."

Well, you better believe I started flipping through my mental black book trying to figure out who this somebody I already knew was! I came up with nothing – blank, zilch, zero! There was not one man I could think of who matched what the pastor said. But for some reason I couldn't explain, I believed what he said; in fact, I clung to every word! I just knew deep down inside that what he said was true!

After all that waiting I had been doing, one year seemed short! I had a whole wedding to plan with this mystery man. I know that sounds crazy, but that is exactly what happened. I started ordering wedding stuff and reaching out to wedding vendors for information. I know some of them must have thought I had lost my mind. I didn't have a wedding date, but I prepared as if I did. I didn't even have a man, but I had a word from God.

You know, sometimes we can miss the supernatural because we're looking for the spectacular. What I mean by that is when God speaks, He seldom makes a lot of noise. That's why people often miss His guidance. I could have easily dismissed what happened in the church that night, and if I had, I might have missed the timing and the person God knew would be just right for me. Thankfully, I was given a specific time (one year), a purpose (you'll meet your *husband*), and a crucial clue to help me identify him when he showed up (he is somebody you already know).

In the midst of my "wedding planning," I relocated to Houston to pursue my Ph.D. Things were going well, and I was starting to feel like I was coming into my own. Then, lo and behold, who should I get a DM from? White Socks! We hadn't seen or spoken to each other for fifteen years! He had also relocated to Texas to pursue his master's degree, and – get this – he had been searching for *me* all those years! Can you believe that? All that time I had spent waiting, agonizing over when I would meet someone, and that someone had been searching for me the whole time! We'll talk more about that in the next chapter, but just as the pastor had said, we reconnected a year from when the pastor spoke those words over me.

White Socks did not waste any time making his intentions known. He wanted a wife; he recognized me as such, and the rest is sweet history in the making. Is ours a beautiful love story? One thousand percent! But the key and the game changer for me was falling in love with Jesus, my true first love. If that had not happened first, I would not have even been in the church that night and heard the words that changed everything about how I saw marriage and my future husband. And let me remind you of my caveat: the way White Socks and I came together was *exceptional*, and I know beyond any shadow of a doubt that he is the right one for me. But that is not likely the way it will happen for most single women, and that's what I want to talk to you about.

An age-old notion has been floating around the relationship realm for quite some time. It's the idea that somewhere out there in the vast expanse of this crazy, wonderful world lies one single, solitary person destined to be your perfect match forever: aka "the one." In two minutes or less, I can prove that "the one" is nothing more than a romanticized fairy tale that might just be doing more harm than good. Walk with me through this imaginary scenario as I paint a theoretical picture for you to prove my point.

Let's say you meet and decide to marry a man that you're convinced beyond any shadow of a doubt is *the* one, the man of your dreams, the peanut butter to your jelly, your *everything*! You've been waiting all this time for your wedding day to arrive. You planned and prepared and pulled out all the stops to make sure it would be the talk of the town. The wedding ceremony is a dream! You look into each other's eyes, choking back the emotion from all the years of waiting for this very moment, and pledge your vows to each other. There's not a dry eye in the place. Then, after being pronounced "man and wife," you make your way out of the church, showered with confetti by loved ones and well-wishers.

As you make your way, hand-in-hand, to the Rolls-Royce Ghost waiting for you outside, "the one" clutches his chest and doubles over with a gasp onto the cold, marble floor of the church vestibule. There's a flurry of panic as one of the guests, who happens to be a doctor, rushes over and performs

CPR. But it's too late. Within moments, "the one" breathes his last, leaving you a widow before you even get to your honeymoon.

Now, here's the question that will drive the point home. After grieving, healing, recovering, and everything else that needs to happen to restore you to wholeness, *would you marry again*? Hold on a minute! Before you answer, let me remind you that you said the man you married was "*the* one." If he was "*the* one," there could be no other one, right? How cruel an ending it would be to resign yourself to a life of perpetual singlehood, knowing you still have the desire to be married! There is no such thing as "the one 2.0." Nope, if he was "the one," he was *it*, and there will be no other. Do you see the dilemma?

See, here's the thing: by fixating on finding this elusive "one," women often miss out on recognizing real gems standing right before their eyes. They become so focused on this idea of a predestined partner that they fail to see the potential in those who could very well be the 'Adam' they've been longing for. And trust me, ladies, there are plenty of 'Adams' out there. But if you keep holding onto the belief that there is only one "the one," you might just let all the other 'Adams' slip through your ringless fingers.

Here's the truth. God is very much into variety. If you don't believe me, just look around you. He could have made everything black and white, but He gave us a myriad of colors on the spectrum. He could have given us one thing to eat, but we have more options than the grand opening of Tiger Dragon Chinese Buffet. He has given you free will to carefully choose, with His guidance, from a *plethora* of options. So, do you really think that when it comes to finding a partner He has limited you to a selection of *one*? No way!

So, let's shift our perspective. Let's abandon the notion of there being only one man for you on the planet and embrace the concept of the "*right kind* of one." What does that mean, you ask? Well, it means opening yourself up to possibilities and being willing to explore connections with those who exhibit the qualities and compatibility you desire. It means letting go of the pressure to find some mythical, solitary unicorn of a creature and instead focusing on building something beautiful with someone who brings out the best of the best in you. Whoever coined the phrase, "There's plenty of fish in the sea," was right! You have *options*. You just need to make sure that "fish" is good for *you*. If you're a "wild-caught salmon" headed upstream, you already know you have no business hooking up with a catfish!

MARRIAGE SHIFT #19

***Recognizing* the one that's *right for you* is better than waiting for "*the* one."**

Are you ready for another myth shift? How about this one: you become a wife *after* you're married. This one is a bit of a mind-bender because it's only logical to assume that you become a wife *after* the wedding, ring, and marriage certificate, but that's not how the Creator of the marriage blueprint sees it.

Have you ever read this scripture from Proverbs 18:22: "He who finds a wife finds a good thing and obtains favor from the Lord." There are all kinds of goodies in that verse, but I want you to notice something in the first part: "He who finds a *wife* finds a good thing ...." Without getting too technical with the Hebrew meaning of the word that is translated 'wife,' let me just say this: the kind of man God has for you will not be looking for a girlfriend, sugar mama, or chick on the side. He'll be looking for a *wife*. That simply means that there are wifely qualities or characteristics a woman can possess and exhibit long before she ever gets a ring on her finger.

Remember, in an earlier chapter, we talked about the power God has given the woman to take whatever vision and purpose God has given to the man (husband) and to incubate, cultivate, and produce more than he ever could on his own. The Bible says, "he who finds a wife finds a good thing," not he who finds a *woman*, but he who finds a *wife*. A man doesn't find a woman and *make* her a wife. He finds a wife and marries her! That being said, according to the Word of God, a man will know his wife because he found what he was looking for. That does not mean you get to play wifey without a legit wifey title. I'm saying that you *become* a wife before a man marries you. Simply put, you *prepare*.

Contrary to what many believe, being "found" is not a passive process; it's a two-way street. To "find a wife" implies that the man is *looking* for a wife, which means a woman should be *recognizable* as a *wife.* You might be wondering why that good man didn't find you. It may be that he didn't recognize you. Be recognizable.

Secondly – and here's the two-way part – it also means that you need to find out what a man wants. Gone are the days when you just *Tee! Hee!* your way through dinner dates. You need to ask *questions.* What does he want you to be in his life? Ask him! *What are you expecting from me? From the relationship?* You need to know what he expects from you as his potential partner. The answer to those questions will tell you if this is some joker who will just waste your time or the kind of man whose vision and purpose you can invest in and work with to build a future together.

MARRIAGE SHIFT #20

A woman is a wife *before* the wedding.

And let me throw another quick one in for free. If a man ever tells you that he wants you to "make him the happiest man in the world," run – do not walk – to the nearest exit. *Why, Karen?* I'm about to tell you.

The problem with marrying a man who wants you to make him the happiest man on earth is he's starting off with the wrong focus. Again, it's in the blueprint. I'll show it to you. Deuteronomy 24:5 says that a newly married man should focus on making his wife happy. It even goes as far as to say that he should dedicate a full year to just that one goal. I paraphrased the verse, but you can read it for yourself.

Now, you tell me: when did anyone ever tell you *that*? Guess what the verse *doesn't* say? It doesn't say *anything* about the wife making the husband happy. That may sound selfish, but when you understand God's design, it makes *perfect* sense. Remember, God made you the incubator – the receiver – and empowered you to multiply what you receive and give it back to your man (husband). Do you see where I'm going? So if the man makes his wife happy, what do you think his good wife will do for him? She won't have to be told to make her husband happy. She'll make him happy *by design*!

Is it fair that the husband be tasked with such a responsibility? One hundred percent! It's to his benefit. In fact, if he follows the blueprint and makes sure his wife is happy, his happiness is guaranteed. Why is it guaranteed? (You are asking some good questions today!) It's guaranteed because God made the husband the leader in the order of the marriage, which means, there's no way he can lead *you* into happiness and not get there *himself*.

MARRIAGE SHIFT #21

Marry a man who wants to make *you* the happiest woman on

earth, instead of a man who wants you to make *him* the happiest man on earth.

Did you know that your happiness as a wife is the thermostat for your husband's prayer life? Let me explain what I mean with another paraphrase of scripture. In 1 Peter 3:7, it says if a husband does not take the time to understand the needs and sensibilities of his wife and take them into consideration, he might as well stop praying because God will not hear him. So, if a husband does not treat his wife right, his prayers are hindered, ineffective, disrupted, obstructed, and cut off! He could be a bishop, pastor, doctor, lawyer, or Indian chief. It doesn't matter. God wants you properly taken care of and *happy*!

MARRIAGE SHIFT #22

When God wants to know how a marriage is doing, He looks at the heart of the wife.

I know we got a little heavy into the scriptural stuff, so let me throw some more practical, everyday truth into the mix. Let's talk about the 50/50 marriage. The short version is *there's no such thing*. But let's go a little deeper.

There's a scene in the move *Jerry Maguire* where the husband rushes into a room full of women and makes himself completely vulnerable in hopes of getting his wife back. With tears in his eyes and his voice choked with emotion, he ignores the stares of the other women and fixes his eyes on his wife as he sputters out one of the most memorable lines in the movie.

"You – *complete* me."

It's an award-worthy moment in the movie, but that line needs to be qualified before it's applied to marriage.

A husband and wife complement each other; they do not complete each other. A wife is the missing piece to her husband's puzzle. At the same, a broken puzzle piece will not complete a whole puzzle, and a broken puzzle cannot be completed by a whole piece. Both the puzzle and the piece need to be whole to properly fit together. Let me put it another way: in marriage, two halves do not make a whole. It takes two *whole* people to make a marriage work. Fifty-fifty is a myth! Both partners need to be one hundred so that it's not only about what you can do for me but what each can bring to this covenant partnership that will make it the best it can be.

MARRIAGE SHIFT #23

If you aren't both whole, you'll end up in pieces.

Let me share two more myth busters with you before I close out this chapter, and they're related. First, let me tell you about the mirror of marriage, and then we'll touch on the university of marriage. You're here for the shift, right? So, let's go!

One of the most challenging seasons in marriage can happen in the "honeymoon" or newlywed phase. As one proverb goes, "Seeing me and living with me are two different things." When a couple marries, their eyes open to things they might not have been aware of before. One of the things that make newlyweds struggle is the realization of imperfection. After the gold dust settles from the honeymoon, you begin to realize that you're living with a man who was "formed from the dust of the ground," and he probably still has some dirt on him. In other words, *he's not perfect*! And guess what? Neither are you.

Marriage is a mirror that shows you things you may not want to see about "him" and yourself. This comes as a shock to most people, but think about it. What would any of us walk around looking like if we never looked in a mirror? It's necessary to face the truth about ourselves even when it's truth we don't want to know. Otherwise, we can never improve and become the best version of ourselves. Would you like it if someone pointed out the big piece of spinach lodged between your teeth? Probably not. It might be embarrassing or, depending on how they told you, even hurtful. But would you be better for it? Absolutely. So, it's not enough for him to always look at you and tell you how beautiful and wonderful and fine you are. That's the part of the "mirror" we like. But sometimes, he'll need to tell you about the spinach in your teeth. And that's okay.

MARRIAGE SHIFT #24

God will use your marriage to show you *you*.

Marriage is one of the most humbling experiences you'll ever have, and that's part of what makes it so wonderful. It's not about your husband humbling you or you humbling him; it's about you humbling *yourself*. That brings me to my final point for this chapter: marriage is a university.

Humility is all about being teachable. When you're teachable arguments end (or never start). When you're teachable blame-shifting is replaced with self-examination – not looking for faults, but recognizing areas for improvement. When you're teachable, you can afford to be more gracious and forgiving when your husband messes up. Why? Because you know that you sometimes mess up too, and you're both growing together.

My amazing husband and I have been together for years, and it still feels as fresh as if we just met yesterday. We have a beautiful life together, but we didn't start from here. We had to grow together. You see, God will use your marriage to perfect your character, and that does not always feel good.

MARRIAGE SHIFT #25

If you're not teachable, you're not leadable.

As I said in an earlier chapter, love does not sustain a marriage; knowledge does, and sometimes that knowledge comes through hard lessons. But those lessons are necessary for you to grow or to see how much you've grown and learned. Knowledge that is not tested is like a treasure left buried; its true worth remains unknown until it's brought to the surface through examination and application.

We all have – what I call – "rocks at the bottom of the glass." When you enter marriage, the glass is full. Then, as you deal with the challenges that undoubtedly come as two previously independent people start to function as an interdependent unit, you pour out of that glass, and the irritations are exposed. While everything is fine and dandy, your rocks (and his) are safely immersed in wedded bliss. But as you pour out by simply carrying out your individual roles as husband and wife and adjusting to each other, those "rocks" start to surface.

This is one reason why having God at the center of your marriage is so important. You need Someone you can each go to when the rocks start showing. God is the only Person who knows everything, so be teachable. Being teachable is simply acknowledging that there is still room to know more. And an unwillingness to learn is the cause of many breakups. So, leave room for the possibility – the reality – that you do not know everything, and let your heart be open to improvement.

Throughout this book, I've been praying for you, and will continue to do so. But right now, I want you to shift and start praying for yourself. Don't worry; I'm not going to throw you out there all alone and leave you hanging, trying to figure things out on your own. I've put a prayer here for you, but it's important that *you* say it, because the investment in your marriage starts now while you're still single. This is a prayer that you can revisit and tweak as you need to time and time again, even after you're married. And what better way to start than with a conversation with the One who made you. At the end of the day, I won't be there when you make that shift into marriage, but He will.

A PRAYER FOR MYSELF

Dear God,

Here I am with an open heart. I've been dreaming about this thing called marriage, but I need You to help me to be ready and hold me through all the highs and lows this journey has to offer. I don't want to sound like I've got it all figured out because, let's be honest, who really does? So, as I prepare for this new chapter, I pray that You fill me with strength and faith and keep me calm and clear-headed as I take my next steps.

I'm not perfect, but help me to be teachable. I trust in You knowing that even when things get tough, even when I feel overwhelmed, I can come to You and talk to You about anything and everything. So, I pray for unity in my future marriage, that we work together, lift each other up, and find joy in every shared moment. Here's to the journey, Lord — the ups, the downs, and everything in between.

Amen.

SAY THIS TO YOURSELF:

I am strengthened by faith, ready for love, and perfectly teachable. Me and God — we got this!

Chapter 5

Why Wait?

"Will I ever find someone to love?"

That question weighed on my mind like a cliffhanger for your favorite season finale, especially after my breakup with The Guy. (Remember him? Yeah, me neither.) I was so traumatized by that messy relationship that I literally asked God to drop my husband in my lap. I believed someone was coming, but I didn't know who or when. All I knew was I didn't want to date, so that left only one other option: *wait.*

Initially, telling people I was "waiting on the Lord" was just a copout – my little hideout where I could run to get away from people who I felt were pressuring me about getting married. But as the wait got longer and longer, there was no place to hide, at least not from myself, and I started wondering if "waiting on the Lord" was even a thing.

Is there really such a thing as waiting on the Lord, and do you get what you're waiting for? I had a lot of doubts and downtimes along the way and moments punctuated with crying sessions. At times, I was on such an emotional rollercoaster; it felt like I was breaking up with the guy I hadn't even met yet! I bounced between feeling fine one day and feeling just hopeless the next.

Thankfully, I did have some things that preoccupied my mind and my time. I traveled with my church choir, hung out with friends, worked on getting my master's done, read books, and took that time and opportunity to get closer to God. It was a bittersweet season in my life, experiencing personal and spiritual growth while at the same time wondering, *Is it ever going to happen for me?*

Getting married and having children was a big dream for me, which is ironic because it's not like I had good role models or examples to follow with my parents. Based on what I had seen and experienced growing up, I should have been running away from marriage. But I had the desire, and I knew it had to be a God-given desire. There was no denying it: I wanted to be married, and I wanted it badly.

MARRIAGE SHIFT #26

The only thing harder than waiting is wishing you had.

We live in a microwave generation. We have instant food, instant long nails, even instant hair. We don't like to wait, and waiting for the right kind of man to come on the scene can be challenging. Most of the time, we don't know who he is, sometimes *where* he is, or what he's like. Worst of all, there's always this little nagging thought in the back of our minds: *When he shows up, will he want me as much as I want him*? If we're not careful, fear and doubt can wreak such havoc in our minds that when the right kind of man does show up, we're too insecure to be receptive.

I've learned that you need to anchor yourself in the assurance of *why* you are waiting so you don't jump at the first offer out of desperation. I understand how uncomfortable and anxious you can get when you're waiting and waiting, and you don't understand what's going on or what to expect. When you're waiting, and you don't understand *why* you're waiting, you immediately start to think about what could be *wrong*. Worse yet, you might start wondering what's wrong with *me*? We get uncomfortable, anxious, maybe even fearful because we don't know what God is doing on the other end.

How you handle your wait has a lot to do with *expectation*. For example, if you're waiting to see the dentist to get a root canal done, then your wait might be a fearful or anxious anticipation of *pain*. But if you're waiting for the mailman to deliver a million-dollar check that you know is coming, then your wait becomes a joyful expectation of something good. See what I mean? Both examples involve waiting, but *how* you wait depends on your *expectation*. David said,

I would have lost heart, unless I had believed That I would see the goodness of the Lord In the land of the living.
— Psalm 27:13

Not to sound preachy, but if you feel like you're losing heart and ready to kick this whole waiting thing to the curb and jump on the next train moving, it may be that you're not yet convinced that you'll see "the goodness of the Lord" in the area of relationship and marriage. But the last time I checked, God is incapable of offering you anything but His very best. So, when you're waiting for God to do something in your life, expect the best. You're worth waiting for, and when you *really believe* that God will show up for you, your wait becomes less of a weight.

Oh, I hear you loud and clear. *That all sounds good, Karen, but if the Lord is good and the giver of every good and perfect gift, why doesn't He just bring His good gift and give it to me? Why can't I have what I want now? Why would a God who is so good make me wait?* You've got questions? I've got answers. So, grab your highlighter, and let's talk about some reasons you may still be waiting. Ready for the gems?

Okay, I want to wrap some verses around each of these reasons so you have some Bible backup for what I'm about to share with you. Here's the first one: your wait is to **PROTECT** you. Psalm 84:11 says *The Lord will give grace and glory;* ***No good thing will He withhold From those who walk uprightly***.

Only two qualifications need to be met for God to give you what you want: first, it's got to be *good*, and second, you need to be walking *uprightly*. Let me say this to heave that big ol' elephant out of the room: walking "uprightly" does not mean you always get everything right. It's simply a way of saying that you're on the God team, allowing Him to guide and have input in your life. The mere fact that you're reading this book proves you qualify for this promise.

Now, let's dig a little deeper into the details. To withhold something means to keep it back from you, and the Bible says if it's good and you're walking with God (i.e., allowing Him to provide direction for your life), He will not keep any good thing from you. And since you are that "good thing" He talks about, if the kind of man that's good for you is doing the same, you won't be withheld from him either! So, if you don't *have* the kind of man or relationship you're waiting for, it must mean it's not *good* for *you*.

Before you throw your "but" in there, let me quickly add this caveat: saying that it's not good for you does not necessarily mean that what you're waiting for or desiring is not good, nor does it mean *you* are not good. God's goodness towards you is not dependent on your own goodness. God is good to you because He *is* good. But as the old saying goes, not everything that looks good *to* you is good *for* you. Ask Eve.

Eve made the mistake of a lifetime! God created everything in the Garden of Eden and said, "It's all good." He also said you can enjoy everything freely, but leave the tree of the knowledge of good and evil alone. But then the devil came and deceived Eve into thinking that God was withholding something good from her, and Eve began to doubt God's goodness. She looked at the tree and it looked good to *her*, so she reached for the very thing that God, in His goodness, was trying to protect her from.

MARRIAGE SHIFT #27

Don't reach for what God has already said is not good for you.

That's a lesson for me and you both. Be careful that while you're waiting, you don't reach for what God has already shown you is not good for you. So many women make that mistake. They go for the okey-doke and "reach" for the kind of man that leaves them in heartbreak. You know the kind: the ones that break promises and never do what they say they're going to do; the ones that treat you like they're doing *you* a favor by being in your life; the ones who lie to you and cheat with anything that's warm and has two legs and a heartbeat. Leave those jokers alone! If you don't have what you're waiting for *yet*, tell yourself *I am worth the wait*, and resist the temptation to doubt God's goodness towards you. Stay within the bounds of His protection, even if you don't fully understand *why* it's not good for you.

So let me repeat: God will use your time of waiting to *protect* you from what is not good for you. And listen to this: sometimes it's not good for you, not because the thing you're waiting for is not good, but because it's not good for you *now*! That brings me to the second reason you may be waiting: to **PREPARE** you.

In Jeremiah 29:11 (NIV), [God] says, ***I know the plans I have for you ... plans to prosper you and not to harm you, plans to give you hope and a future***. God has plans for you, but just because His plans are ready for *you* does not mean that *you* are ready for His plans. Okay, this time, I *do* want to get a little preachy. Turn to your neighbor and say, "God had *plans* for David to be king." He anointed him to be king, He appointed him to be king, but David had to wait because he wasn't *ready* to be king. You can be anointed and appointed and still not be ready. There were some things that David needed to go through, some battles he needed to fight *and win*, and some lessons he needed to *learn* before he was prepared to step into the plans God had for his life. The same is true for you (and me too).

MARRIAGE SHIFT # 28

Never step into a plan that you are not prepared for.

God may have plans to make you a multi-millionaire. But He knows that if He allowed you to have that kind of money now, you'd use it to make Gucci, Louis, Dolce *and* Gabbana, Prada, and Balenciaga richer! And before long, you'd be walking around in He-or and Her-sace because you just weren't ready to manage that level of wealth. You have to be *prepared* for the plan. He may have plans for you to take on a certain role in business or ministry. You might think you're ready, but God knows you're not prepared for the pressure and the demand that He knows will be placed on you. God obviously has plans for you to be married (because you have the desire). But He knows that you're not yet ready to enroll in the university of marriage and all the tests and pop quizzes that come along with that. So your time of waiting is a time of preparation.

One thing you need to understand about God is that He will never put you into a position that He has not prepared you for. This principle requires humility to receive because it means you have to make an honest self-assessment and come to the realization that you don't know everything you thought you knew. But if you ask yourself what you *really* know about being a wife, you'll be able to see the areas that God is trying to target for further development.

Let's do a quick review. Waiting is to *protect* you, to *prepare* you, and here's the third reason: waiting helps to **PERFECT** you. James 1:3-4 (NKJV) tells us that ***the testing of your faith produces patience … [so] that you may be perfect and complete, lacking nothing***. *What? Do you mean God wants me to be perfect?* Yes, ma'am! That does not mean that He expects you to do everything perfectly or that you need to be flawless. This is talking about *maturity* (which is what the word *perfect* means in this verse). He wants to *grow us up* before He *blows us up*, and He uses *time* to perfect or mature us.

I have two beautiful children, and neither one of them wants to wait for anything. They want everything right now. Why? Because they're still children and immature. An unwillingness to wait is a sign of immaturity. The childish person thinks I *have* to wait, but a mature person says I *get* to wait. A mature person understands that times of waiting are *necessary* for us to grow up and be mature enough not just to receive a promise, but to know what to *do* with it when you *do* receive it.

MARRIAGE SHIFT #29

If you don't grow up before marriage, you'll blow up after the honeymoon.

It takes *faith* to wait on God for anything. You don't need faith for something you *don't* have to wait for; you need faith for the things you're *expecting* God to bless you with. You need faith for the things you're still *hoping* for. Here's another backup scripture from Romans 8:24 (the last part) and 25 (NLT): *If we already have something, we don't need to hope for it. But if we look forward to something we don't yet have,* ***we must wait*** *patiently and confidently.* The mature person understands that faith cannot be fully developed without patience, and patience *cannot* be developed without times of waiting. It's like an Oreo cookie with the cream filling: you need both parts – faith and patience – for it to work.

Now we've come to the fourth and final reason: your wait may be to **PACE** you. Check this verse out:

Habakkuk 2:3 For ***the vision is yet for an appointed time****; but at the end it will speak, and it will not lie. Though it tarries, wait for it; because it will surely come, it will not tarry.*

Here's the gem: some promises God has for you are *time-released*. And if it's time-released, there's nothing you can do to make it happen any faster. He may or may not choose to reveal to you His timing. *You just have to wait.* If that sounds harsh, it's because you don't yet have an understanding of what an "appointed time" is. So let me explain.

The verse says that the vision is for "an *appointed* time." The word *appointed* there means it is a *set, scheduled time* on God's calendar. One thing I've learned about God is that you can't rush Him. You can cry, get angry, throw a tantrum, and when you're done with all that, you'll still have to wait. Waiting is sometimes necessary to *align* you with God's timing. It sets you at just the right pace so that you are at the right place at the right time to get what He has in store for you.

Understand that God has a *set time* to release certain things in your life. *God never makes you wait for what He's already said no to.* If you don't remember anything else I've said in this chapter, remember this: ***'Wait' is a 'Yes!' with***

a date on it. Don't try to outrun God's timing. Wait on the Lord and trust Him to pace you so that you will be at the appointed place at the appointed time to receive what He has for you. And when you get there, you're going to find that you were not waiting for your blessing; your blessing was waiting for you!

Well, can you believe it? We're almost through this marriage shift, but there's one more area we need to dive into a little deeper. In this chapter, we chatted about *why* waiting is important. Now, we need to roll up our sleeves and get down to the nitty-gritty of the wait itself. Yes, I know that waiting can sometimes seem as exciting as watching paint dry. But trust me, it's a crucial part of the process. But what does it mean to "wait on God?" Is it like waiting for your coffee to brew in the morning? Or is it more like waiting for your favorite artist to drop their new single? And what should this time of waiting look like? Is it a Netflix and chill situation? And let's not forget about *dating*. How does *that* factor into the equation?

Go ahead and get yourself some more snacks, and let's get into this final chapter. (Don't forget a napkin so you don't leave crumbs in the creases of the book. That would just be *wrong*!) We're about to uncover all the juicy details of what this "waiting game" is all about. Ready?

A PRAYER FOR MY SINGLE SISTER ...

Dear God,

I come to You on behalf of my single sister. As crazy as it

sounds, I want to thank You for her wait. Thank You for helping her to see the wisdom of waiting. Thank You that she can trust Your goodness and expect Your best.

I pray that she will not get frustrated, anxious, or fearful while she waits. Help her keep her mind focused on the good things that are coming towards her and to relax. After all, You did say that while You work on us with the tool of patience, we should keep our cool (Luke 21:19). Give her the grace that makes her time of waiting restful and enjoyable. And help her not to get so focused on the promise of marriage that she forgets the Person who made the promise.

Thank You for protecting her from what is not good for her. Thank You for preparing her and helping her to see the areas that still need to be developed in her life. Thank You for growing her up so that she can be mature enough to handle the blessings You have in store for her. And thank You for aligning her with Your timing so she will always be at the right place at the right time.

Amen.

SAY THIS TO YOURSELF:

I am a masterpiece in the making, and I am worth the wait.

Chapter 6

Found

Let's jump right in. Before we get into a discussion about how to date, what's acceptable and what's not, I want to do a part two on this issue of "waiting" on God. Why? Because it's a principle that has been grossly misunderstood. And that is why so many single women are living with disappointment, frustration, insecurity, and flat-out fear that they haven't met and may never meet the kind of man they want to spend the rest of their lives with. So, let's talk some more about this whole idea of waiting and clear away some of the cobwebs that have clouded so many women's minds and outlook on relationships.

The first thing I want to say is waiting is not passive. Take a deep breath and read that one more time. It is not passive, and once you understand what I'm about to share with you, you'll feel a whole lot better about this wait state you've been in. "Waiting on God" has become a churchy, Christianese cliché that has been tossed around like unstrapped furniture in a moving van on a road full of potholes. It's made a mess of people's understanding of a biblical principle that is designed to enhance your life rather than put it on pause. Waiting on God is not about sitting around until a particular time or until something happens. Nope, it's not about that at all. Let me paint a more accurate picture to explain what I mean.

Let's say you're going to get your nails done. You enter the lobby or reception area, and after letting the receptionist know you're there, you take a seat. After a few minutes (depending on how early you got there), your personal manicurist comes out to greet you and takes you back to a private space where all your nail pampering treatment is prepped to begin. She seats you in a comfortable chair, and while you're sipping on a cool, refreshing beverage of choice, she trims, shapes, massages, and polishes your nails into manicured bliss.

Now, with that picture in mind, if I asked who was doing the waiting, you or your personal manicurist, you might be tempted to answer that it was you. But it was actually the manicurist. You see, we have been led to believe that waiting is a passive activity. So, naturally, you would think that waiting for the manicurist to come out or waiting for your nails to get done would posture you as the one who was waiting. But when you understand that, from a biblical perspective, waiting refers to actively *serving*, it gives you a whole new perspective on waiting and your wait in particular.

MARRIAGE SHIFT #30

Waiting "on" instead of waiting "for" removes the weight from your wait.

It's really not a difficult concept to grasp. Let me give you another example. When you go to a restaurant, you are seated, and then someone comes to you, gives you a menu, and you place your order. You are waiting *for* your meal, but you are called a customer or patron. However, the person who is waiting *on* you is called the "waiter." The waiter is not the one who is sitting down expecting to be served but the one doing the *serving*.

It's the same idea regarding waiting for the right kind of person. You're not just sitting around waiting for something to happen. Instead, you're *serving* yourself and others. Your time of waiting can (and should) be spent actively involved in those things that are pleasurable and beneficial to your life and others. What is it you want to do? Do you want to travel? Now's the time: travel while you're waiting. Do you want to start a business, finish school, buy a house, serve in ministry, change careers, volunteer, check items off your wish list – do it while you're waiting on God!

MARRIAGE SHIFT #31

Life does not start with "I do." It starts now.

In the Bible, there's a beautiful love story about a woman who became single again at a young age. Her husband had died, and there were slim pickings as far as available men were concerned. So what did she do? She relocated. She didn't move with the intention of finding someone to be with. She moved intending to serve someone she was close to. She believed that was her best next step – and it was. Her name is Ruth, and her love story is so inspiring that an entire book of the Bible is written about her.

After she got to her new location, she received some advice from her mother-in-law to make herself more visible to a man her mother-in-law believed would be the right kind of man for her. And Ruth followed her advice. Ruth wasn't pushy or obvious, but she didn't hide herself either. She went to work at a business the guy owned, and, sure enough, he noticed her. The rest, as they say, is history.

Let me press pause right here and say this. While it's true that the primary responsibility of finding a wife lies on the man (according to Proverbs 18:22), it's up to the woman to be more *findable.* I can't tell you how many Christian single women I've talked to who want to be married, yet immediately after church, they're the first ones to beat a track to the exit! Even though I asked God to drop my husband in my life, my experience was more the exception than the rule. For the most part, Angel Gabriel is not going to come down from Heaven and knock on your door with a "Here art thou husband!" delivery.

There are simple, practical things you can do to help you be more findable. For example, when you go to church, don't be so quick to run out the door when the service is over. Linger a little bit. Greet a few people, especially if you see a brother who is single, available, and possesses qualities that demonstrate he might be a qualified candidate. There's nothing wrong with being friendly, asking a question, or finding out what they thought about the sermon.

MARRIAGE SHIFT #32

You can't meet a man you're running away from.

And here's a novel idea: *smile*! Do you know the pressure a man is under when he is interested in and wants to approach a potential wife, and her face is as serious as the Grim Reaper? All some men need is a little encouragement to pluck enough courage to make their approach. You'd be amazed at how people will respond to a simple smile. You may be the bright spot of their day. After all, who wants to "connect" with a frowning sour-puss?

If you're looking for ways to add a dash of irresistible allure to your interactions and make yourself instantly more attractive, you already have one of the most potent tools at your disposal. It's not some fancy perfume or a new outfit. It's your smile! *Really? A smile?* Yes, a smile.

In fact, research is on your side. Studies have shown that smiling alters the relationship between attractiveness level and perception. In simpler words, smiling makes you more attractive. *Boom*! Science has spoken. But let's not stop there. Another study found that increased smile intensity contributed significantly to perceived trustworthiness in women. So, not only does a smile make you more appealing, but it also amps up your trust factor. It's a double whammy!

Many women are lowering their necklines and snatching their waistlines to try to attract a guy's attention. Yes, it's true that men are visual, but the kind of man you need is one who is more interested in what's on the inside than what's showing on the outside. And on the flip side of the coin, the perception of your own attractiveness should not be based on how a man reacts or doesn't react to your outward appearance.

MARRIAGE SHIFT #33

Dress the way you want to be addressed.

Your beauty or feelings about whether or not you are beautiful should not be based on whether or not anyone approaches you. That's a dangerous trap that could lead you to change your behavior or appearance to attract a man. There are many women who are "ugly" in nature, character, and behavior who are approached by lots of men. But that does not mean that they are beautiful. Some men are like flies, and we both know what flies are attracted to. How you present often determines who responds.

Don't be concerned with flattery, which is based on what is superficial. The kind of man you really want to attract is one who is more concerned with what he cannot see at a glance: the inner beauty of your character and spirituality. Focus on being the best you can be – inside and out – and the rest will follow.

I was once approached by a twenty-five-year-old woman who wanted to know why it was so hard for her to get a date. That nagging question was pulling down her self-esteem to the point where she was getting depressed and feeling unattractive. All she wanted was to go out and experience "a real date for a change." Maybe you can relate. She was making a couple of critical mistakes. First, she assessed her self-worth based on her dating life (or how much attention she received or did not receive from men). Secondly, she assessed her qualifications based on what she *thought* men were looking for.

The secret to being truly attractive is knowing your own worth. You will discover your worth as you uncover and discover your assets: your gifts, talents, resources, abilities, etc. When you accept as truth what God says about you as His child and an individual with purpose, potential, and power, you will become a magnet for men of quality.

Every woman is moved by words; that's how we're wired. It's one of our strengths, but it can sometimes be our downfall if we're not careful. Some joker comes along and whispers sweet nothings, tells you what your father never told you or what you never told yourself, and *BAM!* You run into a relationship with someone who has learned to use what should be your strength as your weakness.

I remember a classmate I met in college. She was smart, pretty, friendly, *and* nice, but those weren't the things that stood out the most to me. What struck me was how unmoved she was by the many guys who approached her. She exuded self-confidence, and no matter how much flattery she got from her admirers, she would just give them an "I already know that" smile and keep it moving.

After some conversation, I found out why she could not be swept away by any Tom, Dick, or Rahim that came her way and showered her with flowery words. She had already heard them all, or at least the ones that were most significant to her. She grew up with an adoring father who always told her how smart, pretty, and successful she was. So when the fellas came around trying to get that number, there was nothing they could say that she hadn't heard before and that she didn't know and already believe about herself.

Confidence is attractive. But maybe you're like me, and you didn't have anyone to speak into your life and build up your self-esteem and confidence like my college mate's father did. That may have made you somewhat susceptible to smooth-talking guys who only told you what they thought you wanted to hear to get what they wanted. But I'm here to tell you that it's never too early or too late to start speaking life to *yourself*.

MARRIAGE SHIFT #34

Look in the mirror and tell yourself what you want to hear.

You cannot be all things to all people. That is the danger of trying to mold yourself into an image of what you think men might be looking for. The qualities that one man may be looking for may be completely different from what another man may look for. So, the question is not only about what qualities men are looking for, but what qualities you are looking for and developing in yourself. This is crucial when it comes to dating because your view of yourself will determine what kind of boundaries you set.

Boundaries are the mental, emotional, and physical "fences" you put around your life and person to determine who you let in and who you keep out. God (through the writer of Proverbs) tells us that we should guard our hearts. I like the way the Living Bible puts it:

> Above all else, guard your [heart's] affections. For they influence everything else in your life.
> — Proverbs 4:23

The reason why we sometimes experience "broken hearts" is because we let the wrong joker in! Even Jesus knocks at the door of your heart and waits to be let in. He expects you to contemplate the value He can add to your life and then, based on that, decide to let Him in. Shouldn't you do the same with a man who wants to win your heart?

Set a standard for yourself. It's okay to say, "No thank you," or "I'm good" to someone who expresses interest in you but in whom you're not interested. As a matter of fact, it's good to do that because every joker that comes along is a time-waster and a blocker for the right kind of man. Which reminds me of another story.

There was a monkey who, like any monkey, loved nuts. So, a hunter set a trap using nuts as bait, and it worked. The monkey inched up to the jar, reached in, and grabbed a fistful of nuts. The only problem was his hand was so full of nuts that he couldn't remove his clenched fist from the jar. The very things he was holding onto were the things that were keeping him trapped. He did not realize that by letting go of the things he was holding on to, he would set himself free. What's the moral of the story? *Let go of the nuts*!

There's something even better than releasing those people, habits, and cycles that trap you in situations you need to get out of, and that is not getting into them in the first place. That requires boundaries. Now, I need to say this:

setting boundaries does not mean keeping your heart locked up because of past hurts. Boundaries require you to sit down, take inventory of your life experiences, and decide what you will or will not allow into your life moving forward.

So, how do you know you've found the right kind of person? This is more a question of faith than recognition. Faith is having an assurance now of what you expect to get in the future. And faith has to be *specific*. You can't just say I want a "good man." You have to be specific about what that "good man" is like. How tall is he? What age or age range? What level of education does he have? What sort of career: is he white collar, blue collar, business owner, or entrepreneur? Does he have a beard, or is he clean-shaven? Has he been married before or not? Does he have children? How much money does he make? Can you be that specific? *Yes, you can*!

MARRIAGE SHIFT #35

In relationships, you'll get what you *expect* or *accept*.

If you don't have any expectations or express your desire only in general terms, how will you recognize the fulfillment of that desire when he arrives? You won't! But if you are specific, you will be able to recognize him. So, you need to sit down and think about the kind of person you would want to be with. There's no need to obsess over it, but when it comes to the characteristics that are most important to you, you should have a clear idea. That's not something anyone else can decide for you.

When we want a car, we think about what features we want it to have, the color, price range, make, and model. We have no problem doing that for a hunk of steel that we'll likely only keep for a few years. How much more important is it for you to sit down and think about the kind of person you want to spend a lifetime with?

Another part of recognizing the right kind of person involves *time*. One of my favorite quotes is, "Time has a big mouth. If you give something enough time, it will tell you everything you need to know." I know you want to move closer to the wedding vows, but *take your time*, even when you believe the right kind of person has come along. Don't let anyone rush you into a marriage you might not be ready for. Trust me, the right kind of man will wait and allow you time and space to be sure that he is the one you really want.

Most importantly, pray for God's will. He promised to give you direction if you include Him in the process (see Proverbs 3:5-6). At the same time, it's important to understand how God's will works. I like to think of the will of God like an automatic door, like the kind they have at the supermarkets. When you approach the door, there is a mat in front of it or a sensor near it that triggers the door to open, but nothing happens until you step on the mat or come into the range of the sensor.

Most people who want God's will walk up to the mat, but they never step on it, so the door never opens, and then they wonder why. Here is a simple formula to use inspired by Proverbs 3:5-6: "**Trust in the Lord with all thine heart; and lean not unto thine own understanding. In all thy ways acknowledge him, and he shall direct thy paths."** It reads even better in the CEV translation: **With all your heart, you must trust the Lord and not your own judgment. Always let him lead you, and he will clear the road for you to follow.**"

So, here are three simple steps.

1. **Don't trust your own judgment**. Recognize that you're capable of making wrong decisions, and ask the Lord to help you recognize the right kind of person when they come along.
2. **Always let God lead you**. Trust that He'll do what He says, which is to give you a clear, straight path to follow.
3. **Step on the mat!** With His promise in mind, move forward confidently without fear of mistakes, mishaps, or missteps.

Relationships require a great deal of emotional involvement, particularly of women. They take a lot out of you, even more so if you become sexually involved. The sexual act is not just physical; it's spiritual. A connection is formed at a much deeper level than skin-to-skin, especially for a woman. That is why when a woman has been sexually involved, it is much more painful and difficult for her when the relationship ends.

Let me drop this potent fact that you may not have heard of. It has been scientifically proven that the DNA of every sexual partner a woman is involved with is passed through the man's semen to the woman's children. If you doubt what I'm saying is true, ask Professor Google. *Time Magazine* published an article on how previous sexual partners affect offspring. So, in reality, women who have had multiple partners and refer to a particular man as their "baby's daddy," should more accurately say, my "baby's *daddys*!"

I know that's some deep stuff, but it gets even deeper! There are psychological and other effects of having multiple sexual partners. I'll just drop one more and leave it here: when a woman is sexually involved with a man, not only is his DNA powerful enough to travel into her future and alter any children she might have, but his DNA is also powerful enough to physically change *her*! For example, a woman's hair texture can change because of the man she messed with. Now that's some deep, eye-popping stuff!

Also, most men don't marry the woman they "play" with. He may keep coming back for more, but a sexual relationship with him undermines his trust in you. Some women pride themselves on how good they are in bed, not realizing that the man is secretly wondering, "Who taught her *that*?" And without realizing it, that woman has undermined any hopes of having a marriage built on trust with that man. What you choose to do with your body is entirely up to you. But what I have shared with you is a worthy consideration.

Know your worth. You might feel like a hidden diamond waiting to be discovered, and that is a good analogy. To the untrained eye, the worth of a diamond is not readily seen. Some of the men you'll meet may not be able to see the worth of a diamond in the rough, but that does not make you any less valuable. God sees you, and He knows your worth. Allow Him during this precious time of waiting to polish you up and put the facets in all the right places. If you leave that process in the hands of men, you may end up cracked or chipped away to nothing. The more you work on yourself, the more your brilliance will become uncovered.

Let the Master Diamond Cutter work on you until you become the brilliant gem you are destined to be. When you're shining, you will be more easily found. And, if you stay close to the Master Jeweler, He will see to it that the person who finds you can appreciate the process and the pressures you've endured as a diamond in the rough, and who can fully appreciate and value the uniqueness and individual beauty that is yours and yours alone.

I hope you've enjoyed our journey together. Hey, do me a favor: drop me a note to let me know how your shift is going, and send me a picture of your wedding day when the time comes. I can guarantee you that as you follow the guidance I've shared with you for your marriage shift, you will be smiling as you walk down the aisle *and* step into your wonderful marriage.

A PRAYER FOR YOU ...

Dear God,

I just want to take a moment to celebrate my sister's journey. She's been on a path, one that has led her to explore the depths of her soul. As she steps into the next phase of her journey – her future marriage – I ask for Your blessings. Bless her with a drama-free relationship where respect and understanding are a given. Guide her with Your divine direction so that she may choose a partner who will not only love her but also lead her closer to You.

Give her discernment to see beyond the surface, to recognize the heart that aligns with hers, and to understand the soul that resonates with her own. Remind her always of her worth, that she is precious in Your eyes, and should settle for nothing less than a love that recognizes and celebrates her value.

Let her find joy in the present moment, knowing that every step of her journey is a part of Your master plan. Let her find peace in the future, knowing that Your plans are always for her good. Let her find love, always and in all ways because she is love, and she deserves to be loved in return. Thank you, Lord, for hearing this prayer. We trust in Your timing and know that the best is yet to come.

Amen.

SAY THIS TO YOURSELF:

I am destined for a drama-free relationship and a love-filled marriage that makes me feel like the queen I am.

Acknowledgments

I thank the Holy Spirit for curating a blessed and amazing life and marriage for me. I owe Him everything!

I am thankful to my husband, who supports and encourages me to be the person God wants me to be. I am able to accomplish so much because of his love, consistency, wisdom, and godliness.

My daughters are my biggest supporters. They have shown me how to love in a way I never thought possible. I am eternally grateful to God for blessing us with them.

My sisters Stephanie and Jennifer, my biggest encouragers and therapists, lol – I'm so grateful God made us sisters. You inspire me daily to push beyond the limits and embrace endless possibilities.

I thank my coach and mentor, Aleathea Dupree (The Millionaire Writer), for helping me achieve a dream I never thought would happen. I'm thankful for her guidance, wisdom, and patience. (I can be a bit much, lol.)

Last but certainly not least, I must thank my mom, my biggest inspiration. She taught me everything I know and trailblazed many things I now do, such as writing books and interceding for others. Her steadfast prayers have definitely shaped me into the person I am today. She told me she never had a good marriage but ensured I would have a good one through her unwavering and fervent prayers.

About the Author

Karen Oke is an author, prophetic intercessor, faith catalyst, and Christian life and relationship coach. She is well-known for her best-selling book *The Reluctant Caregiver: Making Peace with An Imperfect Parent*. Her passion lies in inspiring and encouraging people to grow in their faith and strengthen their relationship with Christ.

Karen has a BA in Psychology and a master's in Clinical Social Work from the prestigious New York University. With over twenty years of experience as a licensed psychotherapist, Karen has helped countless individuals through circular therapy. She now focuses on helping people on a spiritual level, recognizing that it serves as the foundation for all other aspects of their lives.

Guided by the Holy Spirit, Karen is called to reveal the will of God, activate destinies through prophetic intercession, and establish the Kingdom of God within the hearts of men and women. Also an enterprising entrepreneur, she is the founder of Original Plan Apparel (OPA), a faith-based lifestyle brand.

Karen has been blissfully married for fifteen years and is a dedicated mother to two amazing daughters. When she's not writing books or changing the world one life at a time, she loves making things pretty as a wedding and event planner, bringing joy to others on their special days.

Connect with Karen at www.karenimalaministries.com

Also by Karen Oke

The Reluctant Caregiver: Making Peace with An Imperfect Parent

Available on

Amazon.com

Barnes & Noble

Available now wherever books are sold.

Milton Keynes UK
Ingram Content Group UK Ltd.
UKHW020815260224
438492UK00015BA/691

9 798987 7517